To Eileen 2021
with love & laughter
Margie

Laugh Lines

Getting Old Is Funny!

Written By Alison Pohn

new seasons™

Stanley, I think they've changed to smaller stools since we were last here.

Ed's smile turned to a frown when he realized his wife had said "steaks," not "shakes," for dinner.

Here's a tip:

Cabana suit on.

Chin up.

Earl could never figure out why Lena was always so refreshed after an afternoon of errands in town.

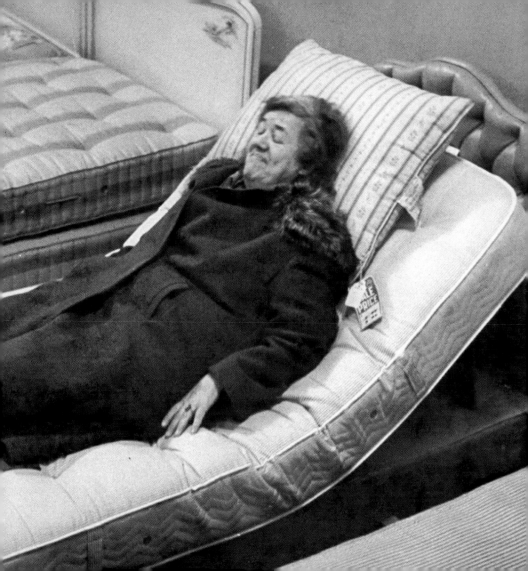

Sure, it wasn't the Chippendales, but the women of Shady Springs Retirement Home appreciated the effort.

Mary-Kate and Ashley,
consider this a warning.

Myra decided to revisit the issue of hormone replacement therapy.

Oh, sure. You're

fooling everyone.

By her 13th grandchild,

Ida had become pretty laid-back.

Men. Who needs 'em?

Being beautiful is hard work.

—Eleanor, how did you get
those shapely thighs?
—Why, walking 10 miles
to and from school,
uphill both ways,
you silly girl.

I've got those falling down arches,

can't see without my glasses,

I hate gravity blues.

Oh, great. This means my husband's at home walking a fried chicken.

Don't get excited.

I'm only checking

my balance.

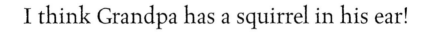

I think Grandpa has a squirrel in his ear!

"Be good and you will be lonesome."

—Mark Twain

Careful, Marshall, or you'll end up with both sets of teeth.

My body's a temple—the temple of doom.

The girls liked to park it right outside Starbucks and taunt the clients with real, percolated coffee.

Remember when your
daily workout was more than
just tying your shoes?

Margie remembered—albeit too late—

where she'd put the leftover rice pudding.

Helen slept on,

secure in the knowledge that

no one else on the bus

remembered where they

were going either.

Cute babe.

Awesome blue rinse.

Don't look. Okay, quick, look!

Fifty-two Christmases,

fifty-two house dresses.

Are you sure this is

the fountain of youth?

Take the picture already.
We're wrinkling like
prunes in here.

Don't mind me.

I'm just sitting here

working out my

retirement plan.

It's nothing fancy—

just my address.

Kings of the

Wild Frontier, indeed.

Oh, no dear. We don't want to buy insurance. We just wanted some company.

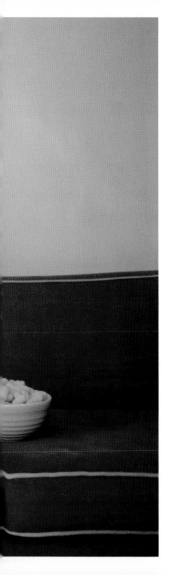

Stayin' alive!

Stayin' alive!

Beauty really is skin deep.

This one . . .

This one's about the

size of my prostate.

Why, I believe this gum

is older than we are!

Girls still wanna

have fun.